Embroidery Magic: A Journey Into the Art of Hand Stitching

Ciarraw N. King

Introduction

Welcome to the world of hand embroidery! This comprehensive guide will provide you with essential information, techniques, and tips to help you master the art of hand embroidery. Whether you're a beginner or have some experience, this guide will equip you with the knowledge and skills to create beautiful embroidered pieces.

We'll start by covering the basic information on hand embroidery, including common misconceptions and the reasons why learning hand embroidery is a valuable skill. Understanding the fundamentals will give you a solid foundation to explore the various aspects of this art form.

Next, we'll dive into the tools, fabrics, and threads you'll need for hand embroidery. We'll discuss embroidery needles, hoops, scissors, and the different types of threads available, such as stranded cotton embroidery floss, metallic thread, pearl cotton, rayon floss, and more. You'll learn which materials are suitable for different embroidery projects and how to choose the right ones for your desired outcomes.

One of the most important aspects of hand embroidery is mastering the stitches. We'll introduce you to essential embroidery stitches, including backstitch, running stitch, stem stitch, split stitch, chain stitch, French knots, and many more. Each stitch will be explained in detail, accompanied by step-by-step instructions and visual references to ensure you can practice and perfect them.

In addition to stitches, we'll explore different hand embroidery techniques that can be used to create unique and textured designs. These techniques include crewel embroidery, pulled thread embroidery, drawn thread embroidery, cross stitch, huck embroidery, cutwork, blackwork embroidery, ribbon embroidery, punch needle, and hardanger embroidery. You'll have the opportunity to experiment with these techniques and discover your personal style.

Transferring embroidery patterns onto fabric is an essential step in hand embroidery. We'll discuss various pattern transfer methods, such as using dressmaker's carbon paper, heat transfer pens, water-soluble stabilizer, tracing paper, hot iron transfers, and pouncing. You'll learn how to choose the right method for your specific project and achieve accurate pattern transfer.

To get you started on your hand embroidery journey, we've included a selection of beginner-friendly projects. From Thanksgiving napkins and flower wall art to embroidered T-shirts and canvas bags, these projects will help you practice your stitches and techniques while creating beautiful and functional items.

Starting and finishing your embroidery correctly is crucial for a clean and professional look. We'll provide you with starting and finishing techniques, including knotting on the back of the fabric, holding stitches, away waste knot, folded thread, holding stitch, and anchoring methods. These techniques will ensure that your embroidery stays secure and tidy.

Lastly, we'll offer maintenance tips to help you preserve your hand embroidery items. You'll learn how to wash them properly, remove stains, test fibers and dyes, avoid sunlight damage, provide proper storage, and more. These tips will help you enjoy your embroidered pieces for years to come.

So, whether you're looking to start a new hobby, enhance your embroidery skills, or create thoughtful handmade gifts, this guide has everything you need to begin your hand embroidery journey. Let's dive in and discover the joy of creating beautiful hand-stitched designs!

Contents

Chapter 1: Basic Information On Hand Embroidery 1

Misconceptions About Hand Embroidery 1

Chapter 2: Why Learn Hand Embroidery..3

Chapter 3: Tools, Fabrics, and Threads for HandEmbroidery 5

Embroidery Needles 5

Embroidery Hoops 8

Embroidery Scissors 11

Stranded Cotton Embroidery Floss 12

Metallic Hand Embroidery Thread 13

Pearl Cotton 14

Rayon Floss 15

Crewel Yarn 15

Tapestry Yarn 16

Silk Threads 16

Cord and Beading Thread...17

Cotton 18

Linen 18

Denim 18

Canvas 19

Wool 19

Chapter 4: Hand Embroidery Stitches You Need ToLearn....................21

Backstitch 21

Running Stitch..22

Stem Stitch 23

Split Stitch 25

Chain Stitch 26

French Knots 27

Lazy Daisy Stitch 29

Seed Stitch 30

Satin Stitch 31

Feather Stitch 32

Couching Stitch 34

Blanket Stitch 35

Fly Stitch 37

Woven Wheel Stitch 38

Chapter 5: Hand Embroidery Techniques 41

Crewel Embroidery 41

Pulled Thread Embroidery 41

Drawn Thread Embroidery 41

Cross stitch 42

Huck Embroidery 42

Cutwork 43

Blackwork Embroidery 43

Ribbon Embroidery 43

Punch Needle 44

Hardanger Embroidery 44

Chapter 6: Embroidery Pattern Transfer Methods 45

Dressmaker's Carbon Paper 45

Heat Transfer Pens 45

Water-soluble Stabilizer 46

Tracing Paper 47

Hot Iron Transfers 47

Heat Transfer Pens and Pencils 48

Pouncing 49

Chapter 7: Hand Embroidery Projects to Get YouStarted...................51

Project 1: Thanksgiving Napkins 51

Project 2: Flower Wall Art...53

Project 3: 3D Satin Stitch on a T-shirt.........................57

Project 4: Embroidery on Necklaces 59

Project 5: Felt Embroidered Bookmark.......................62

Project 6: Embroidery On Shoes 66

Project 7: Embroidered Denim Jeans Pocket.............70

Project 8: Sunflower Embroidered Canvas Bag 73

Project 9: Embroidered Cushion Cover 77

Project 10: Embroidered Napkins With Cutwork 81

Project 11: Ribbon Wall Embroidery Art 84

Project 12: Embroidered travel pouch 88

Project 13: Embroidered Notebook 90

Project 14: Embroidery Hoop Clock 93

Project 15: Embroidery Fridge Magnets......................96

Project 16: Embroidered Photo Art...............................99

Project 17: Embroidered Sunglasses 102

Project 18: Embroidered Medal Patches....................105

Project 19: Embroidered Flowers And Owl Fabric 108

Project 20: Embroidered Scarf.....................................111

Project 21: Embroidered Watch 115

Project 22: Embroidered Seaweed Art 118

Project 23: Embroidered Christmas Tree with LED....123

Project 24: Hand Embroidered Dandelion 125

Project 25: Hand Embroidered Handkerchief 128

Chapter   8: Hand Embroidery Starting andFinishing Techniques 131

Knot On The Back Of The Fabric 131

Holding Stitches 132

Away Waste Knot 133

Folded Thread 134

Holding Stitch 134

Anchoring Method 135

Chapter 9: Maintenance Tips For Your Hand Embroidery Items 136

Hand Wash Them 136

Carefully Remove Stains 136

Test the Fibers and Dyes 136

Soak Instead of Scrubbing 137

Avoid Direct Sunlight 137

Give Them Room to Breath 137

Avoid Acid Contact 138

Avoid Using Starch 138

Dry Them Flat 138

Avoid Ironing the Front Side 138

Chapter 1: Basic Information On Hand Embroidery

Hand embroidery is simply the art of adding decorative stitches on clothing or fabric and accessories using needles, thread, and beads.

You may wonder, "from where did this beautiful handicraft originate?"

Many historians believe that hand embroidery works originated from China and the Middle East, whereby people used stitches to join animal skins to embroider clothing.

In the year 1000, the practice became popular in Europe as the church grew and the royalty gained power. In this case, richly embroidered apparel and accessories like wall art and tablecloths were a sign of wealth and power as only the rich could afford them.

However, it was not until around 1900 that hand embroidery gained more popularity and stopped being a thing for only the rich, as artisans could now use cheaper materials for decorative stitching.

Today, you will see embroidery on a wide variety of items such as dresses, hats, caps, wall hangings, overlays, etc., as well as being available in a variety of yarn colors.

Misconceptions About Hand Embroidery

Here are some debunked myths about hand embroidery.

Myth 1: You must have natural talent and creativity to embroider

Creativity is in everyone, but the difference comes with how much effort and practice we put into bettering our art. I believe that our imagination and ideas are inspired by exploring the world or even looking at stuff others have created to come up with something better or new. For example, your ideas can draw inspiration from exploring nature, which can help you develop new ideas. However, the most important thing is to keep practicing to polish and grow your embroidery skills.

Myth 2: There is no need of learning embroidery

Embroidery may look as simple as working with a needle, hoop, and thread, but the reality is that the process requires you to be patient and master the skill to complete an embroidery project successfully.

For example, you must learn different stitching methods, which are many to complete your designs, which may take some time. However, that does not mean you have to be perfect at first, as there is always time to improve with more practice.

Myth 3: Embroidery is expensive

Some stores may sell materials and tools that are quite expensive, but that does not mean you have to purchase them right away. Starting small is also an option.

For example, for starters, you can purchase second-hand tools that work like new ones or even use fabrics that you no longer use in the house. You can slowly purchase new fabrics and tools as you progress with time.

Myth 4: Embroidery is boring

There's nothing boring about seeing your designs come to life. Besides, embroidery is no longer used on clothing and accessories alone but also on wall art. Imagine having wall art created by you! Isn't that thrilling?

Chapter 2: Why Learn Hand Embroidery

Here are a few reasons why:

Provides entrepreneurial opportunities

If you have an entrepreneurial mindset, you can create new and unique hand embroidery styles, which you can transfer into clothing and accessories and then sell them. This requires that you be very creative with adequate embroidery skills that can attract your target market.

Besides, online market platforms such as Amazon, Facebook marketplace, eBay, Etsy, and many others have enabled people to sell their items digitally, making it easier to target a bigger audience.

It is a handy skill

Imagine you have a torn tent or canvas for camping or other needs in your store. Will you dispose of it? The answer is no because here is where your embroidery skills come in handy.

Learning how to embroider reduces the cost or need of having to buy a new tent or canvas because you can repair the torn part by simply creating a design around it. This idea may also apply to torn garments!

It is a form of tourist attraction

In 2014, researchers conducted a study[4] to assess how the people of Taal, Philippines perceived the embroidery industry. The study concluded that the practice largely benefits the country's tourism industry and creates employment for many.

Since hand embroidery expresses different cultures from different regions, people from foreign countries buy these embroidered items as souvenirs of the places they have visited, promoting the embroidery industry.

Creates employment

Hand embroidery can create a living for you, solving job problems for many. Some designers may need your skills in decorating their designer garments and accessories uniquely, which could be a job opportunity for you if you have a creative mind and the skills required.

Also, some online stores that sell embroidery items can create a job opportunity for you by helping you gain more online sales.

It is unique

With technology, embroidery overall has evolved with people using machines and computers to embroider their items. But that is not so for hand-embroidered items, which remain unique as they reflect the artist's creativity and feelings.

It is therapeutic

From history, war soldiers from Australia, New Zealand, and Britain were encouraged to practice hand embroidery as part of their post-war therapy to help them recover their mental skills and overcome the war trauma. You did not know that, did you?

Hand embroidery is a form of therapy as it keeps us away from our daily worries and chaotic thoughts as we concentrate on the artwork. It is like meditation, making it beneficial and good at improving your emotional and mental health.

Now that you understand what hand embroidery entails, let us see what tools, threads, and fabrics you require for your projects.

Chapter 3: Tools, Fabrics, and Threads for Hand Embroidery

Here are the tools you will need for your hand embroidery projects:

Embroidery Needles

Needles help you draw the thread through the fabric when embroidering. However, when it comes to hand embroidery, you do not require just any needle available in the store. You need to use the right needle for the job to ensure you deliver better results, especially if you are a beginner.

Below are the different types of embroidery needles;

Crewel needles

This needle has a sharp tip that has a medium-long eye which tends to be slightly larger than the needle eye.

Milliner needle

Also known as the straw needle, the milliner needle has a sharp tip, a long shaft, and a short eye that is almost round.

Tapestry needle

The tapestry needle has a longer eye than the crewel needle and a shorter shaft than the latter. It also has a blunt tip that allows it to work easily with embroidery that includes laces or whips without snagging the stitches.

Beading needles

If your project involves beadwork, then a beading needle is what you require. It has an extra small eye and a long shaft. Also, this needle comes in handy when threading small holes in your project.

Embroidery Hoops

An embroidery hoop helps you keep the fabric tightly pulled or taut when embroidering so that your stitching does not pucker, resulting in a warped-out embroidery.

To use one, you loosen the screw to separate the outer and inner hoops, then place the hoop without the screw flat on your work surface. Next, evenly place the fabric on the hoops by pulling on all sides of the fabric and continue adjusting the screws until the fabric is nicely taut.

When purchasing embroidery hoops, go for the plastic or wooden ones, especially if you are a beginner. These hold the fabric well, and there is no warping.

Round embroidery hoops

These are round in shape and are available in different sizes, which you can choose from depending on your project. Examples of round hoops include plastic round hoops, height-adjustable round woven embroidery stand hoops, and round wooden embroidery hoops with an iron stand.

Oval embroidery hoops

These have an oval shape, and you can use them in cases where the design is longer lengthwise.

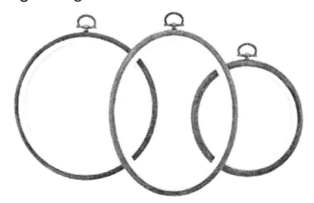

Square hoops

If your design is square, you can use square hoops to guide you when stitching.

Triangle hoops

If you have a triangular design, you can use a triangle hoop.

Slate embroidery frames

Using this frame is advantageous because you can easily embroider with both hands as the frame comes mounted on stands. Also, it makes it easy to work on large pieces of fabrics and large designs as it has a large frame.

Embroidery Scissors

Note that these scissors are different from regular scissors as they have smaller and thinner blades that are usually very sharp and look pointy at the top when closed.

You should use these scissors instead of the regular ones because they provide a clean cut of the threads as they get close to the fabric. Here are different types of scissors;

- **Straight tip**: These have very slender blades and fine points that cut close to the fabric.

- **Curved tip**: These scissors have slender, curved blades at the tip, and the points are very fine; hence, they cut close to the fabric.

- **Steeple tip**: They have a curved blunt tip and a sharp blade that gets under the fabric without ripping it.

- **Hook-blade**: With these scissors, you can easily get under one stitch and cut close to the embroidery; you can also use them for clipping stitches from the reverse side.

- **Bent handle**: They have a straight blade parallel to the embroidery work though the handle is made so that it is above your work.

- **Snips or clips**: They have short blades and come with or without a finger hole. You can use these scissors for clipping threads or yarns.

- **Applique scissors**: They have a unique shape and allow for cutting close to the fabric without ripping the fabric.

Thread-wise, you can choose from the different types available depending on your project.

Stranded Cotton Embroidery Floss

Like many others, you may also prefer to use cotton embroidery thread as it has a soft twist and texture and allows for more freedom when you are embroidering. It also has six strands that you can thread together to your needle or separate the strands depending on the effect you want for your project.

If you want delicate and fine lines, you can thread one strand on your needle; if you want thick lines, you can thread your needle with up to six strands.

Metallic Hand Embroidery Thread

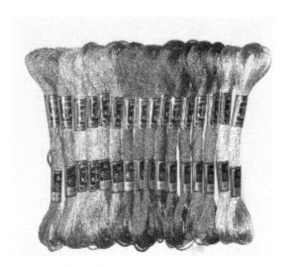

As the name suggests, the thread has a metallic spark that adds a pretty decoration to your fabric. You can use metallic threads to provide highlights to your embroidery work or use it on their own.

To work with this thread, use short strands instead of long ones and fewer strands. Also, use bigger embroidery needles and often trim off excess floss.

Pearl Cotton

This thread is slightly heavier than the stranded cotton embroidery floss thread and is available in many weights. It also has single strands made of two fibers twisted together and not meant to be separate.

You can use this type of thread for cross-stitch, redwork, or to make beautiful tassels which are cords of threads hanging loosely and knotted on one end for decorating clothing, furnishings, drapery, etc.

Rayon Floss

Because of its shiny and bright colors, you can use rayon floss to make a beautiful impression on decorative quilts or appliques. However, you may find that it is a difficult thread to work with since it tangles easily. Thus, it is best to use short lengths of the thread to avoid these problems. You can also dampen the thread a little by running a wet cloth to moisture it, which effectively keeps the tangles away.

Crewel Yarn

Crewel yarn is a fine thread made of natural wool and consists of two-ply strands. You can use it for needlepoint, cross-stitch, tapestry work, or wool embroidering. Also, you can use it for projects that need texture as the strands are thick enough.

Tapestry Yarn

This yarn is usually thick and soft, and you can use it on heavy materials like canvas. You can also use it for needlepoint projects, crewel embroidery, and cross-stitch.

Silk Threads

Silk thread is perfect for your project if you want to show off stitches in your embroidery work. Silk thread is available in different beautiful shades you can use to highlight your embroidery work.

However, silk threads fade easily and bleed when washing, so after you are through with your embroidery work, lightly press the back of your project using a steam iron with slight steam.

Cord and Beading Thread

If your embroidery projects involve any beadwork, you can get nylon thread to make the beading stitches since they are strong, durable, and usable with fine beads. You can also use waxed cotton cord thread and polyester stretch cords since they are thicker and more durable.

Next, let us look at fabrics we can use.

Cotton

As a beginner, going for a 100% woven cotton fabric is a great option, as it tends to have a tight weave that works well with a variety of stitches. It also comes in a wide variety of colors and is affordable.

Linen

Linen has a great texture that can give your embroidery work a rich look. When purchasing the fabric, try going for 100% linen as it is tighter and does not stretch when stitching.

Denim

Denim is heavy-weight with a twill texture, making it great for embroidery hoop art. Embroidery hoop art is art embroidered within the hoop and displayed either on walls or any part of the room. If you have a pair of old denim clothes you want to dispose of, you can cut up the fabric and make embroidery hoop art items.

An example of a denim hoop art

Canvas

Canvas fabric is cotton-made but is heavier and sturdier. Working on it may seem a little difficult for the first time, so try stitching with a sharp, large needle and thicker thread to make your stitching work easier.

Wool

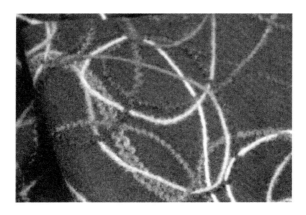

If you have ornaments, appliques, or accessories as part of your projects, then wool is ideal as it does not stretch or have a weave. When embroidering using wool fabric, use six strands of cotton embroidery floss or pearl cotton thread so that the threads may stand out on the fabric, which has a fuzzy texture.

Next, let us look at the stitches you need to learn for hand embroidery.

Chapter 4: Hand Embroidery Stitches You Need To Learn

As a beginner, you need to learn the following stitches:

Backstitch

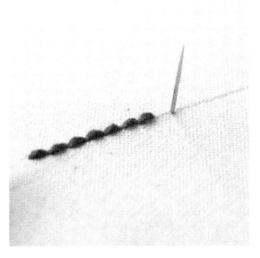

Here's how to do a back-stitch;

1. First, bring your thread up from the back and pull it through, then do one stitch forward.

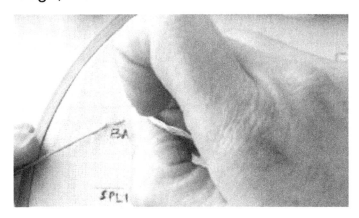

2. Next, pull the needle through from underneath, making sure to space the needle according to your desired stitch.

3. After that, bring the thread and needle back down through the end of the stitch you just made, making the back-stitch.

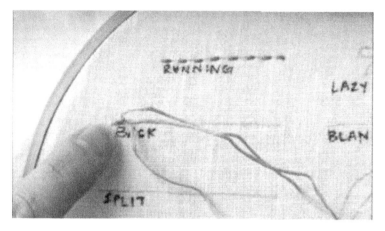

Running Stitch

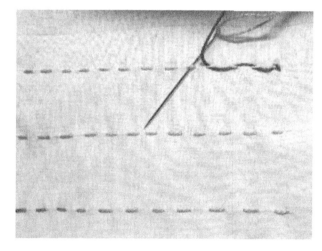

Here is how to make the running stitch:

1. Start by bringing your needle and thread up through the back of your fabric, then move one stitch length forward

back to the back of your fabric.

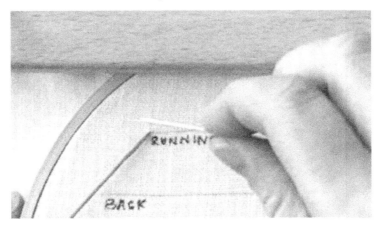

2. Next, bring the needle back up and move another stitch length forward, creating even space between the stitches. Keep doing this until done.

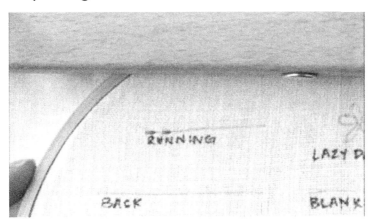

Stem Stitch

1. Start by bringing your needle and thread through the back of the fabric, then move one stitch length forward but before you pull the thread all the way down, bring the needle up at the middle point between the stitch length and pull it all the way up.

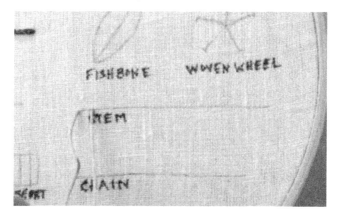

2. Next, move a shorter stitch length forward, but before pulling the thread all the way down, bring the needle up right through the hole where the first stitch length went down into and pull the thread all the way up. Keep doing that until you are through with stitching.

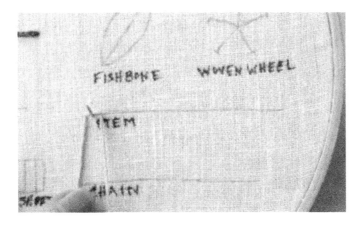

Split Stitch

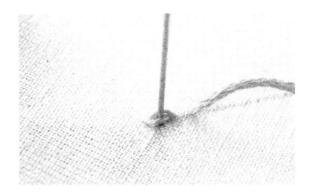

1. Start by bringing your needle from the back and pulling the thread all the way through to the front.

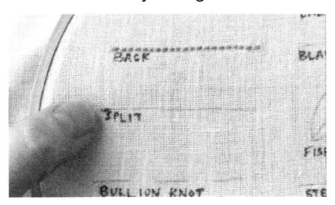

2. Next, move one stitch length forward and pull all the way through downwards.

3. Next, bring the needle up through the middle of the previous stitch, move another stitch length forward and bring the needle up through that stitch. Keep repeating the same motion until done.

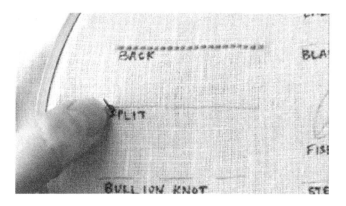

Chain Stitch

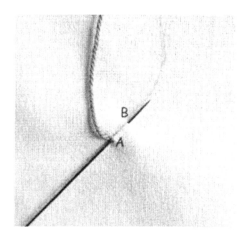

1. Bring your needle up through the back of your fabric and then bring it back down right through the very hole you pulled it up through, leaving a loop there.

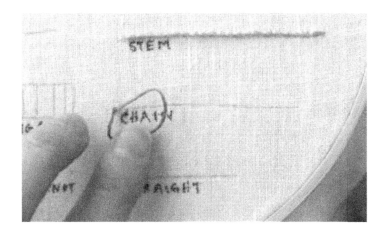

2. Next, go one stitch length forward from the back, bring your needle through the loop you created, then pull through, making sure the stitch is not too tight.

3. Next, move your needle down through the hole you came up from inside the last stitch, and leave a loop. Move up one stitch length forward, making sure the thread comes up through the center of the loop, then pull all the way through but not too tight. Repeat the motion until the stitch is complete.

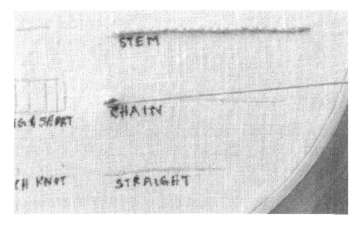

French Knots

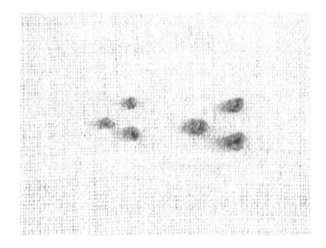

1. Start by bringing the needle up through the spot where you want your knot. Take the needle and point it away from your work and wrap the thread around the needle twice.

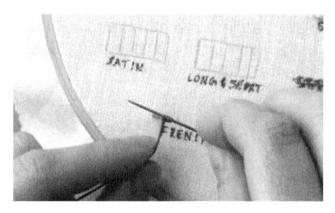

2. Next, take the needle back through the same hole you brought it up, ensuring you are holding the thread tightly, then pull it all the way through to the back.

3. Next, bring your needle up again through the back and follow the same steps. The spacing of your knots depends on the design you are creating.

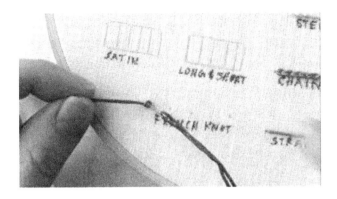

Lazy Daisy Stitch

1. Bring your needle up through the pointed end of your shape and then take the needle through the same hole, leaving a loop.

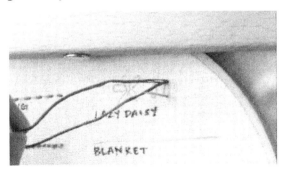

2. Next, bring the needle through the end of the curved end, making sure it goes through the loop, then pull the thread but not too tight, forming a teardrop shape.

3. Next, bring your needle a little bit forward from the hole you just brought your needle back up from to secure the curved end of the shape. Keep doing that until all the shapes are complete.

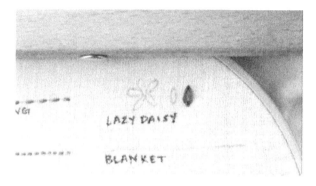

Seed Stitch

1. Bring the needle up through the back of your work and move a short stitch length in any direction that you desire.

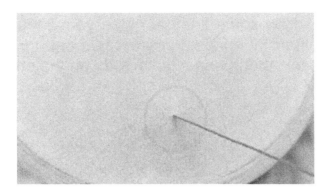

2. Keep your stitches as random as possible, ensuring they are uniform and the white space between them is almost the same. Keep doing that until done.

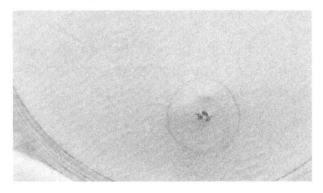

Satin Stitch

1. First, draw some lines to guide you when stitching. After that, start by bringing your needle and thread up through the back, then bring it down through the other end.

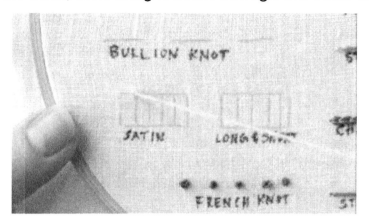

2. Next, bring the needle up through the back of the fabric again and keep stitching through the lines until you have filled in the shape of your design.

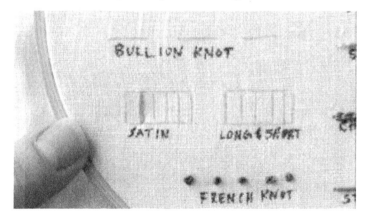

Feather Stitch

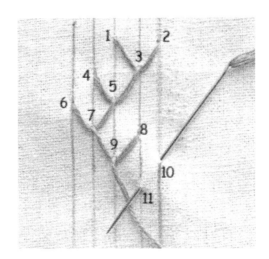

1. Start by making parallel lines depending on the size of your pattern. Next, bring your needle and thread up on the left end of the top line, skip one of the parallel lines, and bring your needle down still on the left side, leaving a loop on top of your fabric.

LOOPED   BUTTONHOLE   TURKEY
BLANKET   WHEEL

FEATHER

HERRINGBONE

2. Next, go one stitch length forward on the line between the two lines, then bring your needle up, making sure it goes through the loop.

3. Next, bring your needle to the bottom line, leave a loop and move up one stitch length to the right in the middle of

those two lines through the loop to form a V-shape.

4. Go back to the top line, bring the needle through to the back, leave a loop, move one stitch length forward to the right on the line between the two lines through the loop, and tug it again to form a V-shape.

5. Continue doing that down the line until your pattern is complete.

Couching Stitch

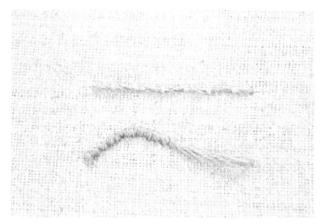

1. Start by bringing the first thread through from the back and lay it in any direction.

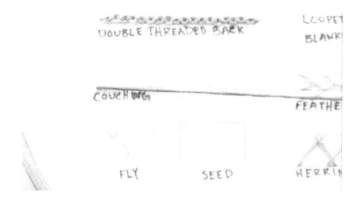

2. Next, bring your second thread and needle from the back and a stitch length forward from the first thread.

3. Make a small stitch over the first thread using the second thread and needle so that it tacks it in place.

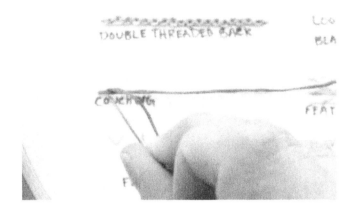

4. Keep bringing the needle up and down to make stitches, so the first thread is tacked, making sure the space between the stitches is even.

Blanket Stitch

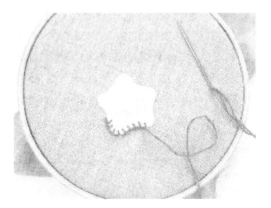

1. Bring the needle and thread through the back of your fabric, then move one stitch length towards the diagonal right creating a loop.

2. Next, bring your thread back up one stitch forward in line with the first hole through the loop you created and tag it a little tight to form an L-shape.

3. Next, bring your thread down in line with the diagonal right hole, leaving a loop, then bring your thread up in line with your bottom lines and again tag to form another L-shape.

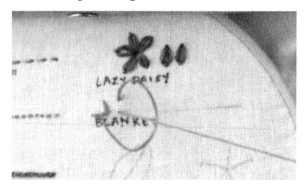

4. Keep doing that until your design is complete.

Fly Stitch

1. Start by pulling the needle through the top left of the v and bring it down through the top right, leaving a loop.

2. Next, bring it back up through the base end and pull the needle all the way through, forming a V-shape. Make a small stitch to secure the v in place. Keep doing that until your embroidery is complete.

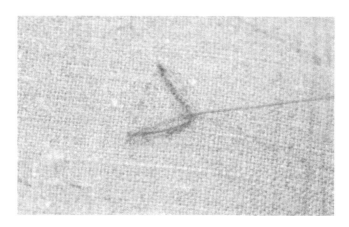

Woven Wheel Stitch

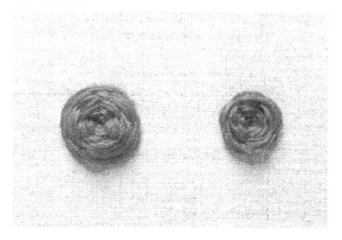

1. Start by sketching the outlines so that they make a wheel. Next, bring your needle up from the end of one of the lines and bring it back down through the center. Continue doing that for all the lines.

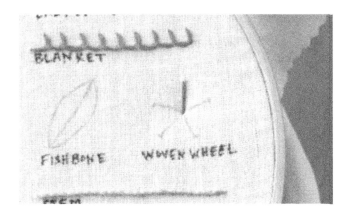

2. Next, bring your needle up near the center and start weaving a pattern around the center. To do this, bring the needle under one of the threads and over the next thread all the way around. Keep alternating the threads you are going over and under.

3. Do this until the wheel is completely covered in thread.

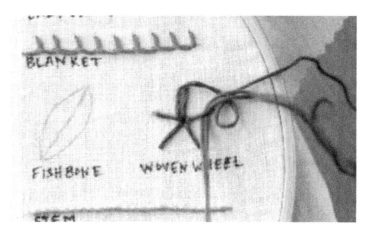

With the stitches covered, let's now focus on technique:

Chapter 5: Hand Embroidery Techniques

Here are different types of embroidery techniques you can try out.

Crewel Embroidery

Crewel embroidery is a type of embroidery that exceptionally uses wool thread. Unlike other threads, crewel thread is thicker, creating a raised texture and dimension to the art piece.

When purchasing crewel wool, look for the one labeled as such but avoid mixing different brands since they have different textures. For the fabric, go for the linen and linen twill because they tend to have a close weave which greatly makes it easy to keep stitches in place and sturdy.

You can use any stitching method for crewel embroidery but stick to the crewel needles as they have a large eye for the thread to pass through and have a sharp point that can easily stitch through linen fabric.

Pulled Thread Embroidery

This technique involves creating stitch patterns that pull the fabric's weave, forming holes in the fabric. For this technique, you require a single thread that matches the fabric, a blunt pointed tapestry needle, fabric, and an embroidery hoop to hold your work.

To use this technique properly, Place the fabric with which you are working in your embroidery hoop with the threads lined up at right angles and visible for counting. Also, use a loosely woven fabric that has even weaves like cotton.

Drawn Thread Embroidery

This technique requires removing either vertical or horizontal threads from the fabric by cutting before stitching. After removing the threads, you stitch the remaining threads to hold them in place and make your work more attractive. You can use this technique to make household and church linen.

The best fabric to use is linen because it has an even weave and a tight weave, but you can use any other fabric that has an even weave. There are two methods you can drawback your threads;

- Tie knots on bundles of thread in a pattern.
- Add filling stitches all over your designs.

Cross stitch

This is one of the oldest embroidery techniques. It involves sewing x-shaped stitches together to form a pattern that looks like an image. Because it is easy, you can use different fabrics and threads when using this stitching method.

To cross stitch;

4. First, draw some little squares to guide you when stitching.

5. Bring your needle through from the back of your fabric to the right side of the fabric and at the top left of your square, forming a diagonal line.

6. Bring the needle in a straight line up from the back of the fabric to the bottom left and in line with your first stitch. Your needle should be parallel to where your thread passed through the fabric.

7. Move your thread diagonally across the bottom left and to the top right end crossing the thread from the first diagonal, forming the cross-stitch.

8. Repeat the previous steps to complete the stitching.

Huck Embroidery

Also known as Swedish weaving, huck embroidery is a type of embroidery that combines weaving and a little bit of surface embroidery. It is known as huck embroidery because the common fabric used is huck cloth, mostly used for table linen and towels.

For fabric, you can work with several types, producing different results. Examples of fabric you can use include huck fabric, monk's cloth, Aida cloth, waffle fabric, and popcorn fabric.

For needles, use blunt ones with an angled end as they only pass the thread through the weaving of the fabric instead of piercing it. Also, they make it simple to pass the needle under the floating threads.

For threads, go for stranded embroidery floss and Perle cotton because they both work well with huck embroidery.

Cutwork

For this type of embroidery, you have to cut holes or shapes into the fabric you are embroidering, then hemstitch to decorate the hole's border to keep it from fraying. For example, you can have a teacup shape where you can cut the mouth of the cup and then hem around the cut area to make it look like a real teacup.

Blackwork Embroidery

If you are a black and white enthusiast, you will most likely like this embroidery type as you only use black thread on white fabric by repeating patterns. For the stitches, you can stitch using running stitch, back stitch, and stem stitch.

Ribbon Embroidery

This technique uses silk ribbon, thin woven ribbons, or satin ribbon to decorate the fabric. If you want to embroider flowers or decorate quilts, accessories, or garments, you can use this technique, which is done directly on the foundation fabric.

The good thing is that the style is more of 3 dimensional, making it ideal for flower designs. You can use a variety of basic embroidery stitches for ribbon embroidery, depending on how you are using the ribbons.

Punch Needle

This embroidery type involves pushing a thread or yarn into the fabric using a needle while keeping the needle on the surface, centrally stitching through the fabric. You can use threads and yarns of different weights, ensuring you have the right size of punch needle tools. Your finished project should look chunky from the loops of thread created by your punch needle.

Hardanger Embroidery

This type of embroidery involves cutwork and drawn threads techniques. You wrap thin threads around the warp and weft threads of your fabric, then cut the areas within the embroidered areas to create a lace-like pattern. Make sure to count the weft and warp strands carefully to form the pattern nicely.

Chapter 6: Embroidery Pattern Transfer Methods

There are various ways you can transfer a pattern you want to embroider onto your fabric. Let us take a look at each method.

Dressmaker's Carbon Paper

It's best to use carbon paper for medium-colored fabric or black and dark blue fabric. You can use blue carbon paper for medium-colored fabric such as linen and white carbon paper for black or dark blue fabric.

To transfer the patterns, first lay out your fabric on your work surface, then place the carbon paper on top of your fabric and the pattern on top of the carbon paper. The colored side of the carbon paper should face down. Next, take a pencil or pen and trace out the pattern making sure not to leave out any design detail.

The advantage of using carbon paper is that it washes away easily, while the disadvantage is that it is difficult to trace out.

Heat Transfer Pens

Heat transfer pens are an easy way to transfer your embroidery patterns. You only have to trace the pattern on some paper, then transfer the ink onto your fabric using a hot iron. The ink line is usually very thin, and when you stitch, the stitches easily cover it. However, the ink marks are permanent, so you have to ensure you stitch along the lines to cover them and mark only the areas you intend to stitch.

Water-soluble Stabilizer

When working with dark fabrics, you can use water-soluble stabilizers by just printing the pattern directly onto the stabilizer and then placing it on the fabric. The stabilizer dissolves easily in warm water, so after stitching, you can soak the fabric in warm water, and it will dissolve. However, ensure that the fabric you use is washable and that the thread is colorfast.

Tracing Paper

When using fabrics that are hard to trace onto, such as canvas or any other thick fabric, but you do not want to soak them first, you can use tracing paper.

To use this method, first trace your pattern onto lightweight tracing paper, then baste the paper onto your fabric and stitch through your fabric and paper. Once done with the stitch, carefully remove the baste and tracing paper and clean up.

Hot Iron Transfers

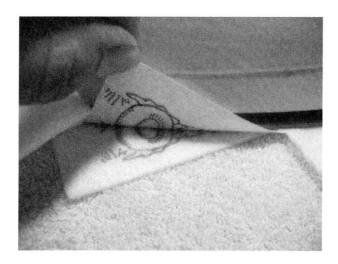

This method uses ready-to-use patterns in various themes and is normally printed in blue, black, and gray. To use hot iron transfers,

1. Have your ready-to-use patterns ready.

2. Place the pattern image facing down onto your fabric.

3. Press onto it using a hot iron to transfer the pattern onto the fabric, and that's it!

Heat Transfer Pens and Pencils

The good thing with heat transfer pens and pencils is that you can use them to mark on both lightweight and heavy fabrics. They are also available in a wide range of colors and thicknesses.

To use them, trace out your design in reverse on lightweight paper so that the mirror image appears on the fabric when you iron. After that, place the paper against the fabric and press it using a hot iron by simply placing the hot iron onto the paper. Avoid moving the iron back and forth to prevent distorting the image.

The disadvantage of using heat transfer pens or pencils is that they are permanent, and the pattern lines do not wash off, so you have to ensure that you cover them completely when stitching.

Pouncing

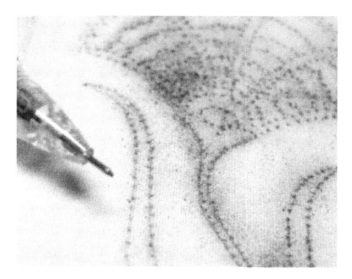

This method involves using a pattern pricked with tiny holes, then placed on the fabric and pounced all over with a powder that goes through the holes, leaving small dots on the fabric. Its use was very prevalent before transfer papers—and other methods—became popular; some people still use it.

To use the prick and pounce method, prick a pattern paper all over or at regular intervals with a pin, then secure it onto the fabric using pins. After that, work the powder pigment through the holes in a pouncing manner using a soft fabric pad. When you remove the paper, tiny dots will appear where the holes were.

Now that you know how to transfer your embroidery patterns onto fabric, let us get started with the projects!

Chapter 7: Hand Embroidery Projects to Get You Started

Here are hand embroidery projects to get you started:

Project 1: Thanksgiving Napkins

Materials

- Napkins
- Heat iron transfer pens or pencils
- Hoop
- Needle and floss

Steps

1. Wash and iron your napkins.
2. Transfer the word patterns onto your napkins using a heat iron transfer pen.

3. Next, grab an embroidery hoop and place the fabric on the hoop.

4. Stitch the letters using stem stitch. Do that for all the napkins.

TIP: Stitching the letters is not continuous; instead of trimming off the thread and starting over, simply move the needle underneath the threads at the back until you get to the point you want to stitch.

Project 2: Flower Wall Art

Materials

- Fabric
- Hoop
- Embroidery floss and needle

Steps

1. Transfer your pattern onto the fabric. Attach the hoop to the fabric and cut the edges of the fabric.

2. Thread your needle with all six strands of embroidery floss and start stitching the petals using both long and short satin stitch. Make the stitches as close to each other.

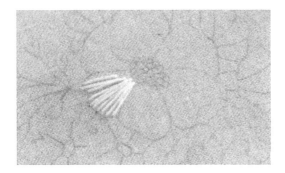

3. Next, stitch the pollens using French knots.

4. Now, stitch the inner petals using a different color floss. The stitches are similar to satin, but you leave a space between the thread and the fabric. Also, fold the thread in half for a thick look.

5. Fold the thread in half to stitch the pollens for the inner petals. Again, leave a space between the thread and the petals.

6. Next, stitch the small flowers using the woven wheel stitch. Do not tighten the thread too much. Also, make a few stitches around the flowers to hide the bottom stitches.

7. Make French knots inside the flowers.

8. Stitch the sepals using satin stitch. Make long and short stitches.

9. Finish with some French knots around the small flowers, and your wall art is done.

Project 3: 3D Satin Stitch on a T-shirt

Materials

- Adhesive felt
- Stabilizer
- Plain T-shirt
- Embroidery hoop
- Embroidery thread and needle

Steps

1. Using regular adhesive, trace the letters out, cut them out, then place them on the stabilizer to form words. Also, put the stabilizer onto the t-shirt and put it into the large hoop so that the whole phrase fits in nicely.

2. Start stitching your cut letters onto the t-shirt using satin stitches with one strand of your embroidery thread. Next, use three strands of thread to fill the letters with different colors, again using satin stitches.

3. Once done, wash the t-shirt to clean off the excess stabilizer, then let it dry and iron.

4. And you are done!

Project 4: Embroidery on Necklaces

Materials

- Fabric
- Tag and bezel
- Glue
- Wooden clamps
- Embroidery thread and needle

Steps

1. First, have your embroidered piece of fabric, bezel, tag, glue, and wooden clamps in place. Refer to steps for project 3 to embroider your fabric or use a custom design.

2. Start by taking your tag and putting it over the top of your design to determine how much fabric you need, then cut about half an inch around the tag.

3. Put the tag behind your embroidery and trim off excess fabric but make sure that the fabric is not too much or too little; just enough is okay. Next, double up the fabric and cut another piece using the original piece, then run-stitch the two together all around, leaving two inches from the end.

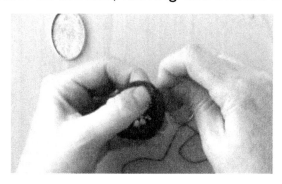

4. Next, give the threads a little tug, take your tag, place it inside the fabric, and tie a knot using the loose threads tightly to secure it.

5. Next, back-stitch anywhere there is a bump on the fabric as shown.

6. Next, smear a small amount of glue around the bezel, then take your embroidery and stick it in your bezel by giving it a nice press down. Make sure the glue does not seep from the sides, then attach the clamps on the sides.

7. Finally, attach the necklace chains, and your embroidery neckpiece is ready!

Project 5: Felt Embroidered Bookmark

Materials

- Carbon paper
- Felt
- Thread and needle

Steps

1. Transfer your patterns onto the felt using carbon paper.

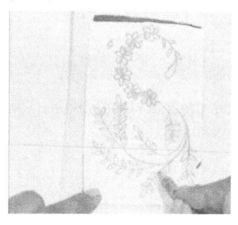

2. Backstitch using six strands of embroidery floss.

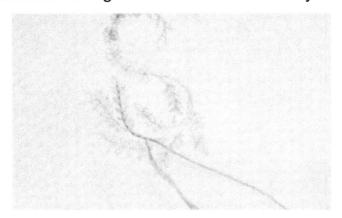

3. For the flowers, use the lazy daisy stitch.

4. Next, make French knots inside the flowers.

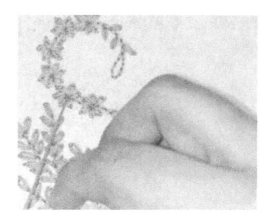

5. Next, make seed stitches for the leaves.

6. Next, cut out a similarly sized felt piece, place it on the wrong side of the original piece, then secure all sides with buttonhole stitch.

7. Secure all sides with buttonhole stitch.

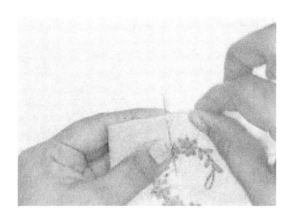

8. And your bookmark is complete.

Project 6: Embroidery On Shoes

Materials

- White-colored pencil
- Sneaker shoes
- Thread and needle

Steps

1. First, sketch your design on the area of the shoe you want to embroider using a white colored pencil.
2. Get your thread and needle and thread it with all the six strands of the floss.
3. Start at the bottom, pull the needle through, then put the needle right where you sketched the stem.

4. Make a fly stitch for the stem and the branches all the way through.

5. Next, make a running stitch for the other branch.

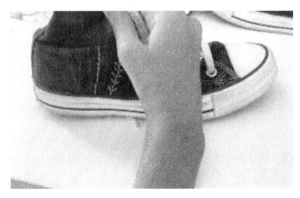

6. Keep making running stitches for the other remaining stems.

7. Next, make French knot flowers along the branches using three strands of thread.

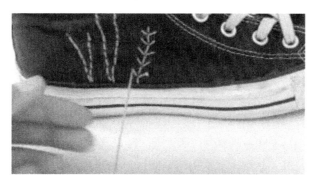

8. Next, make a lazy daisy flower on top of any stem.

9. Next, make an oval French knot flower on top of any stem.

10. Finally, make another lazy daisy flower for the last two stems with some French knots inside the flowers. And you are done.

Project 7: Embroidered Denim Jeans Pocket

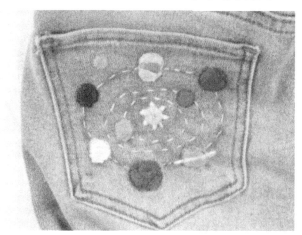

Materials

- Denim trousers with back pockets
- Sketching lead pencil
- Threads and needle

Steps

1. Start by sketching your design on the pocket you want to embroider using a pencil. The idea behind this design is the planets of the universe.

2. Make a woven wheel stitch on the first circle.

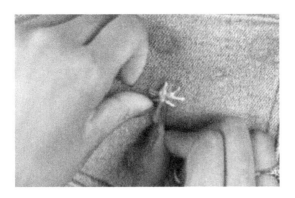

3. Next, fill the second circle using satin stitches and earth planet colors.

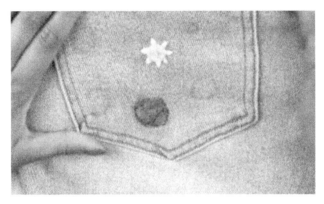

4. Fill the remaining circles with satin stitches using different colors of the planets. Run-stitch around the circles to secure them.

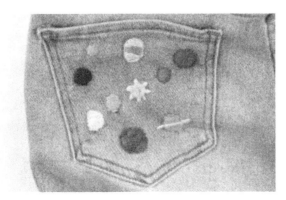

5. Complete the planets by creating short dotted lines around the planets.

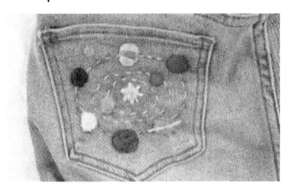

And your pocket design is ready.

Project 8: Sunflower Embroidered Canvas Bag

Materials

- Carbon paper
- Canvas bag
- Threads and needle

Steps

1. First, trace out the pattern onto the fabric using carbon paper.

2. Make a chain stitch for the stem using two strands of green thread.

3. Next, make satin stitches for the left branch and finish by making two small stitches near the branch.

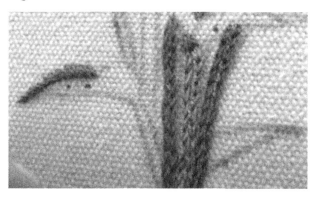

4. Make small stitches starting from the left side of the stem, coming all the way down to the left branch.

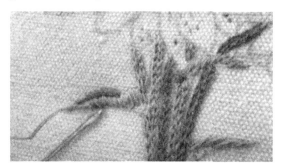

5. Next, start leaf stitching the left leaf.

6. Next, satin stitch the center part of the stalk using three strands of thread.

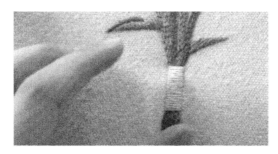

7. Next, satin stitch the flowers using two strands of yellow thread. Make the strands long and short.

8. French knot inside the flowers using four knots of brown and light brown thread.

9. And your canvas bag is complete.

Project 9: Embroidered Cushion Cover

Materials

- Cushion with cushion cover
- Embroidery hoop
- Embroidery threads and needle

Steps

1. First, transfer your pattern onto your fabric, then seal one layer of your cushion into the embroidery hoop, ensuring there are no wrinkles on the fabric.

2. Start stitching the bigger flowers first using the satin stitch and continue until you have filled up the petals.

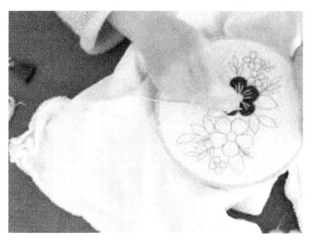

3. Add three simple satin stitches in the middle of each petal to give them an interesting detail. Do the same for both flowers.

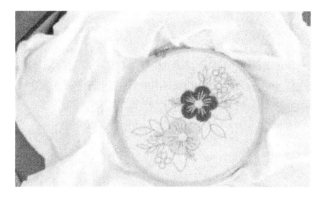

4. Next, stitch the smaller flowers using the same satin stitch method until you fill all the flower petals.

5. Start working on the centers of the flowers by making French knots using differently colored threads. Use four strands of the thread.

6. Next, chain-stitch the small leaves using a different color.

7. Use the same technique on the larger leaves until you have filled in every leaf.

8. Remove the hoop and fit the cushion cover onto the cushion. And you are done.

Project 10: Embroidered Napkins With Cutwork

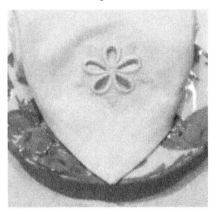

Materials

- Napkins
- Snips
- Embroidery hoop
- Embroidery thread and needle

Steps

1. Start by transferring your pattern onto the fabric. Seal your fabric into the embroidery hoop, ensuring it is tight enough to avoid wrinkling.

2. Take a thread of the same or almost the same color as the cloth and make running stitches along the outline of the flowers.

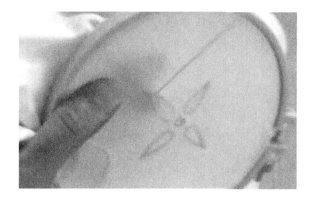

3. Keep doing that for all the outlines of the petals, then take your scissors and snip the middle of each petal vertically. Next, take your needle and thread and make round stitches, ensuring you fully tack in the cut fabric.

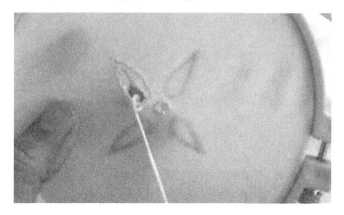

4. Do the same for all petals, and your napkin is ready. Remove the hoop and fold the napkin nicely. And you are done.

Project 11: Ribbon Wall Embroidery Art

Materials

- Ribbons
- Embroidery hoop
- Sketching lead paper or carbon paper
- Embroidery floss and needles

Steps

1. The design idea is an orange tree, so we start by sketching the design onto the fabric using a lead pencil or tracing the pattern using carbon paper. Next, make running stitches for the stem and branches using all six strands of embroidery floss.

2. Next, take your ribbon, pull it through the needle, then make round stitches around the branches and the stems.

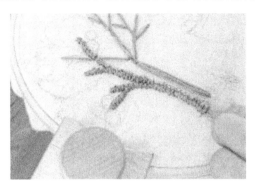

3. Next, take another ribbon of a different color, pull it through your needle, then make stitches for the leaves.

4. Pull another ribbon through your needle and stitch the basket, starting with the vertical lines. For the horizontal lines, stitch through the vertical ribbons going below one ribbon and above the next all the way through as if weaving a basket.

5. Next, take the beads for the oranges and fill them in with thread using all the six strands of thread. The thread must match the color of oranges.

6. Next, stitch the oranges through the branches and the basket.

7. Next, make satin stitches for the flower stems. Make long and short satin stitches.

8. Finally, take another ribbon, pull it through your needle, then stitch the flowers using the lazy daisy stitch.

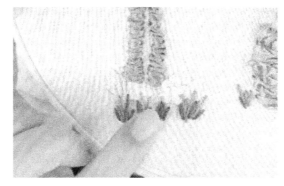

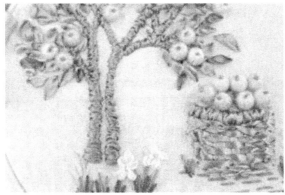

And you are done.

Project 12: Embroidered travel pouch

Materials

- Lead pencil
- Embroidery floss and needle
- Embroidery hoop
- Scissors

Steps

1. First, draw guidelines on your pouch using a lead pencil to help you stitch in a straight line, then thread your needle with two strands of embroidery floss and knot the end of the thread.

2. Sandwich your pouch between the embroidery hoop and start stitching some triangle shapes randomly until you have covered the entire pouch. Use the satin stitching method for the triangles.

3. To give the pouch a more interesting look, add tassels to one end of your pouch. To make one, cut a piece of thread that matches your pouch about six inches long, wrap the uncut thread around three of your fingers depending on how thick you want your tassel, then secure it with the 6-inch-long thread.

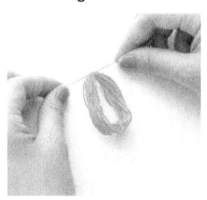

4. Cut another 6-inch-long piece of thread to secure around the wrapped thread about three inches from one end.

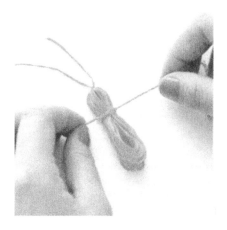

5. Trim the longer end of the wrapped thread to create a fringe.

6.   Attach the tassel to the zipper and your pouch is ready.

Project 13: Embroidered Notebook

Materials

- Carbon paper
- Notebook
- Embroidery threads and needle

Steps

1. Trace out your design using a needle until you have outlined the whole design—if you have a pattern, trace it out using carbon paper.

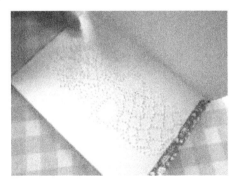

2. Remove the paper carefully and thread your needle with three strands of embroidery thread.

3. Bring your needle through from the back and back-stitch all the way through, making sure to follow the lines you have made to connect the dots. Also, use different colors for a more interesting design.

Project 14: Embroidery Hoop Clock

Materials

- Embroidery hoop
- Clock kit
- Felt and fabric
- Glue and tape
- Ribbon
- Embroidery floss and needle

Steps

1. First, take your hoop, mark 12 equal segments, then use the gap under the tightening screw as the 12-o'clock mark. Separate the inner and outer hoops.

2. Place the felt, then the fabric over the top of the inner hoop, seal with the outer hoop, then tighten the screw. Make sure the fabric is taut.

3. Next, back-stitch the numbers using one or different colors on each of the 12 marks, making sure they are an even distance from each other.

4. Next, stitch the flowers using satin stitch, French knots, and woven wheel stitch.

5. Next, cut out your cardboard disc, insert it in the inner hoop, then cut a small hole at the center to fit the spindle. Glue the disc onto the felt.

6. Next, insert the clock function. Insert your battery pack then followed by the rubber washer on the back, making sure you have the spindle go through the middle hole.

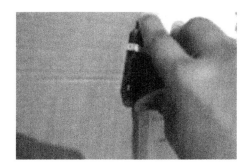

7. Next, fit the hands, the further down the spindle and the minute hand on top. Trim off the excess fabric. And your clock is ready.

Project 15: Embroidery Fridge Magnets

Materials

- Magnets
- Glue
- Cover buttons
- Woven fabric
- Embroidery floss and needle

Steps

1. Transfer the pattern onto the fabric using carbon paper. Seal the fabric with the embroidery hoop, ensuring you adjust it until it is taut.

2. Next, hand-embroider the design using the lazy daisy stitch for the flowers and the back-stitch for the stem.

3. Trace a circle around your design and cut it out.

4. Next, put the fabric face down in your button kit and put the button on top. Fold any excess fabric right into the center of your button then proceed to press all down using a presser to ensure the back is back into place.

5. Glue the magnet to the back of the button and give it time to dry off completely. Do the same for all the other pieces, making sure that they are not close together.

6. After they have dried, stick them on your fridge or cabinets. And you are done.

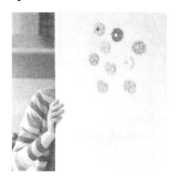

Project 16: Embroidered Photo Art

Materials

- Printed photo
- Embroidery needle and thread
- Adhesive spray
- Cardstock

Steps

1. Choose any photo that has details you can embroider; for example, a cap, sunglasses, mountain, etc., print it out, then spray the adhesive spray to attach your photo to cardstock.

2. Decide how you want your flowers to appear and sketch out the design. In this case, the person is wearing sunglasses which are the center of attention for the wearer. Next, thread your needle with the color of your

choice for the first flower. Stitch using long and short satin stitches for the petals.

3. Stitch all the petals using long and short satin stitches, then make some parallel satin stitches in the center of the flowers using a different color to fill them in.

4. Finally, stitch the leaves using long and short satin stitches to complete the look. You can use different shades of green on different leaves. And you are done.

Project 17: Embroidered Sunglasses

Materials

- Sunglasses
- Drill
- Drill bit
- Scissors
- Thin needle
- Felt tip marker
- Nail polish vanish
- Embroidery floss

Steps

1. Sketch out your pattern on paper, then transfer it onto the sunglasses using a felt tip marker. In this case, the pattern looks grid-like.

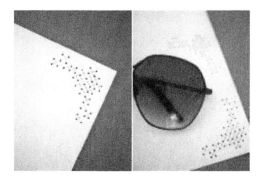

2. Drill holes on the sunglasses using the hand drill, making sure you place the tip of the drill on top of the area you want the holes before the actual drilling to avoid scratching or skidding. After drilling, use the nail varnish to remove any marks leftover.

3. Next, thread your needle and stitch using the cross-stitching embroidery method through the holes, ensuring you follow the patterns. Also, make sure your needle is small enough so that it fits through the holes

4. Keep doing that for all the colors, and finish each color by making a double knot on the backside.

Follow the same instructions for the other side, and your piece is ready.

Project 18: Embroidered Medal Patches

Materials

- Light and dark felt
- Dressmaker's pins
- Safety pins
- Embroidery hoop
- Embroidery thread and needles
- Water-soluble pen
- Scissors

Steps

1. First, transfer your medal patterns onto the light-colored felt using the water-soluble pen, and place the felt in the embroidery hoop for stitching.

2. Next, transfer the patterns on dark felt using the water-soluble pens, and again, sandwich the felt on the

embroidery hoop. In this case, we have used both light and dark felts.

3. Once done transferring the patterns, mark the outlines of the medals, then make running, back, stem, straight, and chain stitches to define them and stitch the other details.

4. Next, use your water-soluble pen to write the texts on the medals and remove the excess ink by submerging them in water, then dry them by hanging them. You can speed up the drying process by pressing them gently with a clean, dry towel.

5. Finally, cut out the medals using scissors, then back them using felt and glue. Apply glue to the back, press a piece of backing felt onto the glued area, then leave it to dry.

Once the glue dries up, trim the edges. And your piece is ready.

Project 19: Embroidered Flowers And Owl Fabric

Materials

- Water-soluble pen
- Muslin
- Scissors
- Embroidery floss and needles
- Embroidery hoop
- Cotton batting

Steps

1. Transfer your design to the fabric using a water-soluble pen. The best way is to have the fabric and the image over a lightbox, then trace out the image. That way, you can see the image clearly.

2. Next, place your fabric over the cotton batting and sandwich the two with the embroidery hoop.

3. Start stitching using the back-stitch, satin stitch, French knots, blanket stitch, and chain stitch.

4. Once done with the embroidery, rinse it under running water to remove the water-soluble pen marks, then hang it to dry, and your piece is ready. You can sew the fabric into a cushion cover or a bed pillow!

Project 20: Embroidered Scarf

Materials

- Cotton scarf
- Embroidery threads and needles
- Scissors
- Lead pencil

Steps

1. First, mark some lines along which you will stitch. You can use a ruler to make straight lines. Arrange your threads in your stitching order to avoid confusion.

2. Start stitching. Start with the running stitch and make two rows.

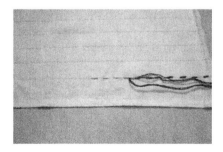

3. Follow with the fly stitch. Make one row.

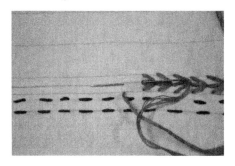

4. Next, make the VanDyke stitch. To work this stitch, bring the needle through the back of the fabric, then make a small stitch at the middle point of the two lines. Next, take the needle through the fabric to make a narrow cross. Bring your needle up below the first stitch, then pass the needle under the crossed threads. Next, take the needle to the back of the fabric on the right side of the line, then bring the needle back to the left below the stitch and repeat the instructions until done stitching.

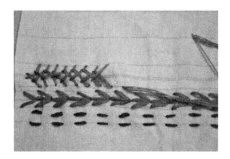

5. Next, make the cross-stitch.

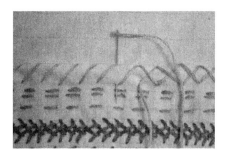

6. Follow with the chain stitch.

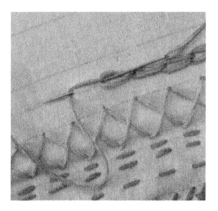

7. Next, make the looped running stitch. First, make the running stitch, then loop the needle along it, as shown below.

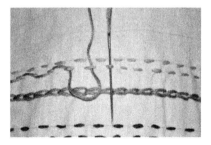

8. Complete with the crossed running stitch. And your scarf is ready.

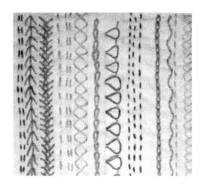

Project 21: Embroidered Watch

Materials

- Watch
- Fabric
- Pencil
- Scissors
- White glue
- Thread and needle

Steps

1. First, disassemble your watch carefully, noting where everything goes to avoid mistakes when reassembling it. First, remove the backplate, followed by the pin, and finally, the watch face.

2. Trace out the watch face on paper using a pencil, then trace out the pattern onto the fabric using carbon paper. It is easier that way.

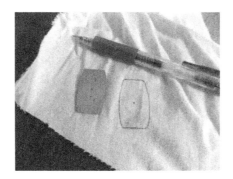

3. Thread your needle with three strands of embroidery floss without tying a knot at the end, then stitch the numbers using satin stitch. After completing this, apply a thin layer of white glue to the back to secure the stitches, then leave it to dry.

4. Next, cut out the new watch face and glue it onto the old face, making sure to press the fabric as flat as possible.

5. Lay the new face into the crystal, then reassemble all the other parts. And your embroidered watch is complete.

Project 22: Embroidered Seaweed Art

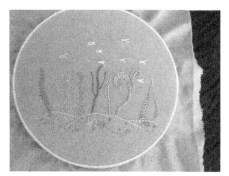

Materials

- Embroidery hoop
- Fabric
- Embroidery threads and needles
- Watercolor pencil
- Scissors

Steps

1. First, have your pattern in place, then trace it onto the fabric using the watercolor pencil. You can print out your pattern or sketch a design.

2. Sandwich your fabric onto the embroidery hoop.

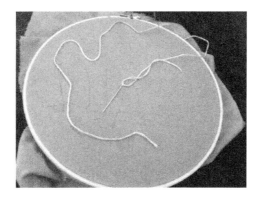

3. Start stitching. Start with the bull's head stitch to represent the fish.

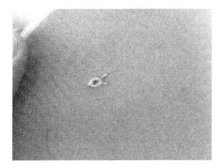

4. Next, make the back-stitch to represent the sand outlines.

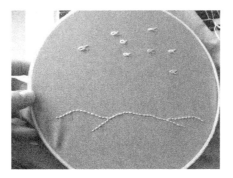

5. Next, make the French knots to represent the sand rocks.

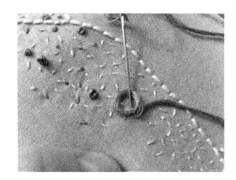

6. Follow this with making the lazy daisy stitch to represent the starfish.

7. Make the barb stitch to represent the first strand of seaweed.

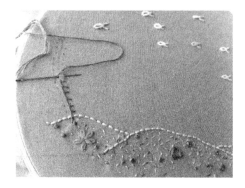

8. Next, make the fly stitch to represent the second seaweed strand.

9. Make the feather stitch to represent the third strand of seaweed.

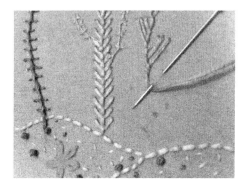

10. Make another feather stitch.

11. Make a coral stitch to represent another seaweed.

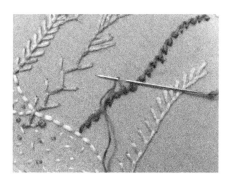

12. Make a chain stitch to represent another seaweed.

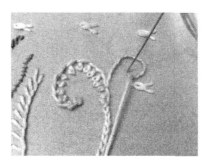

13. Finally, make the stepped running stitch. And your piece is ready.

Project 23: Embroidered Christmas Tree with LED

Materials

- Embroidery hoop
- LED lights
- Embroidery floss and needles
- Pins
- Scissors
- Felt and fabric

Steps

1. First, trace out your Christmas tree pattern onto the felt and cut it out. The fabric must have Christmas colors.

2. Place the fabric in the embroidery hoop and trim off the excess fabric.

3. Next, thread your needle and make a blanket stitch around the tree's outline to secure it onto the fabric.

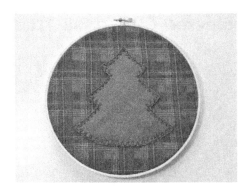

4. Next, attach the LED lights for more decoration. To do it properly, poke holes through the fabric, then arrange your lights with the positive side facing the top of the hoop and the negative side facing the bottom of the hoop. Next, use pliers to bend the lights flat against the fabric and spiral the legs into the loops for stitching. Make a running stitch along the length of the tree. Also, sew the bottom loops of the LEDs to the line. Once done stitching, insert the battery into the holder. And your embroidered Christmas tree is ready.

Project 24: Hand Embroidered Dandelion

Materials

- Embroidery hoop
- Embroidery needle and thread
- Fabric
- Water-soluble pen

Steps

1. Trace out the pattern using a water-soluble pen. Alternatively, you can draw your design directly onto the fabric using the water-soluble pen.

2. Sandwich your fabric in the embroidery hoop.

3. Thread your needle with all the six strands of embroidery thread to get the desired thickness of the leaves. Next, start stitching using straight stitches in between the first row.

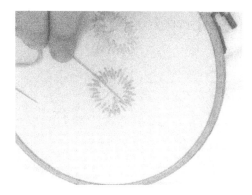

4. Next, use overlapping stitches between the flowers to keep the fabric from showing or to fill in the stitches.

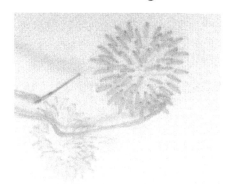

5. Next, use stem stitches for the stem and fly stitches for the leaves.

And your dandelion is complete. You can use it as wall art.

Project 25: Hand Embroidered Handkerchief

Materials

- Embroidery hoop
- Handkerchief
- Water-soluble pen
- Embroidery floss and needle
- Scissors

Steps

1. First, choose the side you want to have the decoration then, draw your design onto the handkerchief using the water-soluble pen. Place the pattern underneath the handkerchief and trace it out.

2. Next, use your embroidery hoop to hoop the fabric by loosening the outer hoop, then sandwich the handkerchief between the inner and outer hoop. Make sure to adjust your fabric so that it is taut when stitching.

3. Next, thread your needle with two strands of embroidery thread, then make one knot at the end. Snip off the excess thread.

4. Start by stitching the letters if you have initials using the back-stitch. For the dot, just make a small stitch. Once done, turn the hop over and tie a knot by passing your needle under the next stitch, hold the thread in your thumb, wrap it around twice, and pull the needle all the way through to make the knot. Trim off excess thread.

5. Next, thread your needle with two strands of a differently colored thread for the plant. Make a back-stitch for the stems and leaves.

6. And your handkerchief embroidery is done. Remove the embroidery hoop and fold your handkerchief nicely.

Chapter 8: Hand Embroidery Starting and Finishing Techniques

In hand embroidery, there are many ways you can finish your stitch, depending on what kind of stitches you use.

Let us look at some of these ways:

First, let us look at the starting techniques;

Knot On The Back Of The Fabric

Simply tie a small knot at the end of your thread after threading the needle, then embroider your fabric, leaving a knot on the back. It is the simplest method, although it has its pros and con;

Pros of using knots:

- You do not end up wasting thread.
- You do not need to add more stitches to secure the thread after stitching.
- It is a simple and quick way to start embroidering.

Cons of using knots:

- When using dark threads or thin material, your knots may be visible from the front side.
- Knots start getting loose with time, resulting in your embroidery falling apart, especially if you wash the embroidered item.
- Knots may not feel irritable on the skin if used when embroidering clothes.
- They make your embroidery work appear unprofessional.
- Knots appear as tiny bumps even on thick materials.

Holding Stitches

A holding stitch is a sequence of small stitches that secure the thread on fabric and are made on the line or within the shape you are embroidering so that it lies under the stitching. To do it,

- Make a knot at the end of the thread and bring the thread down through the fabric.

- Pull the thread all the way through, then bring your needle up next to the knot, either within the shape you are embroidering or on the outline. Either way, the holding stitch must lie under the stitching.

- Pull the thread all the way through, make two small stitches, then bring your needle up where you want to start embroidering and cut off the knot as close to the fabric as possible.

Pros of using holding stitches:

- You do not need much additional thread to make the holding stitches.

- They are not visible after you cover them with stitching.

- It is smooth on both sides of the embroidery.

Cons of using holding stitches:

- Making holding stitches only requires your design to include areas that need filling in or stitches that cover the holding stitches, like French knots.

Away Waste Knot

We call it away waste knot because you must cut off the knot you make at the start. It works well with all types of threads, stitches, and any number of strands with which you choose to work.

To do it;

- Make a knot at the end of the thread after threading the needle, and bring your needle down through your fabric at least about 3 inches from the point you intend to start stitching to make sure the knot falls on top of the fabric.

- Bring the needle up at the point you want to start your embroidery, making sure the path between the knot and the starting point is not in line with your stitching.

- Complete all the stitches, secure the end, pull the knot up, and cut it off as close to the fabric as possible.

- Thread the loose thread at the back of your fabric onto your embroidery needle, then pass it under the back of the stitches and secure it by wrapping it on the back of the stitches.

Pros of using away waste knot:

- The waste away knot tends to be invisible when you secure the loose thread

- It works with many types of stitches.

Cons of using waste away knots:

- This method uses a lot of thread as you need to have an extra 3-inches of embroidery thread for every stitch you start with away waste knots.

- If you do not secure every cut-off knot immediately, it will get tangled under the embroidery stitches, making your work messy.

Folded Thread

First, you need a thread that is twice the length of the thread you want to use. To make a folded thread:

- Cut a long strand of embroidery thread and fold it in half, then thread it into your needle.

- Bring your needle up through the fabric without pulling it all the way through, leaving a small loop on the back of the fabric. Make a stitch on the front of the fabric, making sure the needle passes through the loop, then tighten the thread. This secures your thread to the back without the need for a knot.

Pros of using folded thread:

- It creates an invisible stitching starting point.
- You do not waste thread.
- There is no need for additional stitches.

Cons of using folded thread:

- You can only use this method if you are using paired threads.

Let us also look at the finishing hand embroidery methods;

Holding Stitch

When you complete a stitch, make two tiny stitches at the end, then bring the thread up through the fabric and cut it off as close to the fabric as possible. Other embroidery stitches will cover the small stitches you have made. However, you must note that this method is great for embroidery work with many covered areas.

Anchoring Method

After making the last stitch, take your needle down through the fabric and turn your project over. Move the needle under the back of three stitches, then back-stitch over that last stitch you moved under, and continue threading under the stitches until the needle is covered. After that, pull your needle through and snip the thread off. The good thing about this method is that it works with any stitch type.

Chapter 9: Maintenance Tips For Your Hand Embroidery Items

Here are simple tips to ensure your embroidery items last:

Hand Wash Them

The best way to wash your embroidery items is by hand using soapy water. When your projects are newly completed or in perfect condition, you can clean them a bit or vacuum them, ensuring you cover the vacuum hose to avoid ruining the embroidery stitches.

If the items are heavily soiled, soak them for about 20 minutes in room-temperature water before cleaning to loosen the dirt or stains. Also, make sure that you rinse thoroughly after soaking in room-temperature water.

However, if you decide to machine-wash your embroidered pieces, ensure you turn them inside out to protect the embroidery during the wash cycle. Also, consider putting the garments in a laundry bag before loading them into the washing machine.

Carefully Remove Stains

Some stubborn stains won't come off even after a good soak and wash, for example, blood, rust, grease, and food. The best way to deal with such stains is soaking them for longer or spot-cleaning with an agent. Before using one, make sure the agent you use is meant for that specific stain.

While at it, do not bleach your linen fabrics as this can ruin the fibers and cause them to have a pink or yellow tinge —this includes white linen fabrics. However, if gentle cleaning does not do the trick, you can add a cupful of bleach to the water and soak.

Test the Fibers and Dyes

Not all fibers are washable in soap and water. Thus, before washing any old or antique embroidered items, check the fibers to confirm if they can withstand washing.

Test the fibers by holding the piece you want to wash up to your ear, then gently turning it in your hands. If you hear a crinkling sound, the fibers are breaking, and you cannot wash the item as this will cause further damage.

You should also test your new projects for dye transfer. Dye transfer happens when the fabric bleeds after being soaked in water due to unstable coloring agents.

To test for dye transfer, dip a cotton cloth and gently rub the threads of the embroidery piece. If the cloth picks up the dye, wash the piece or garment only in cold water and rinse it thoroughly until the excess dye comes off before allowing the piece to dry.

Soak Instead of Scrubbing

While scrubbing may remove dirt, it can easily ruin the embroidery threads and your fabric. The best way to remove dirt from any embroidered item is by soaking it in water for a few minutes, then rinsing.

Avoid Direct Sunlight

Direct sunlight damages everything, so keep your projects out of it to avoid damage. Do not be deceived by the fade-proof sign, as the sun always finds a way to damage anything.

Give Them Room to Breath

Do not store your embroidered items in air-tight plastic boxes because it will cause mold to build up, damaging the fabric and threads used to embroider the project. Allow them to have fresh air always, and if you have to store them, use water-proof boxes.

Also, if you are displaying any framed embroidery wall art, avoid using glass or use spacers that allow air to flow between the fabric and the glass, thereby preventing mold.

Avoid Acid Contact

You may have noticed yellowing on your embroidered items that you have placed against a wooden shelf or surface. This happens because acid is present in wood products, whether sealed or unsealed.

You can prevent this by lining your shelves or wooden surfaces with acid-free paper. For larger items such as tablecloths and beddings, protect them from acid in the closets or drawers by sewing a sleeve out of unbleached muslin and slip the rolled beddings or tablecloths into the sleeve, then stand it up in a closet.

Avoid Using Starch

You may want your tablecloth to feel crisp, and so you may wonder, why not starch it before storing it? That may do more harm than good, as starch stiffens the fibers in the fabric, making them break easily when you fold them or store them for long periods.

Also, some insects like moths feed on natural starch, which means if you use it on your napkins before storing them, they will feed on the starch and possibly ruin the fabric.

The best way to avoid these problems is to starch your items right before using them— if you must.

Dry Them Flat

You can take an old sheet or towel, lay it down, then place your embroidered projects on it to dry. If the pieces are large, you can lay them on a sheet on the lawn. This prevents stretching and ruining the original shape of the item.

Avoid Ironing the Front Side

Do not iron your embroidered garment directly onto the front side because you can easily burn the threads. Instead, iron on the backside of the garment and put a piece of clothing over the embroidered area before ironing.

Printed in Great Britain
by Amazon

28762826R00090

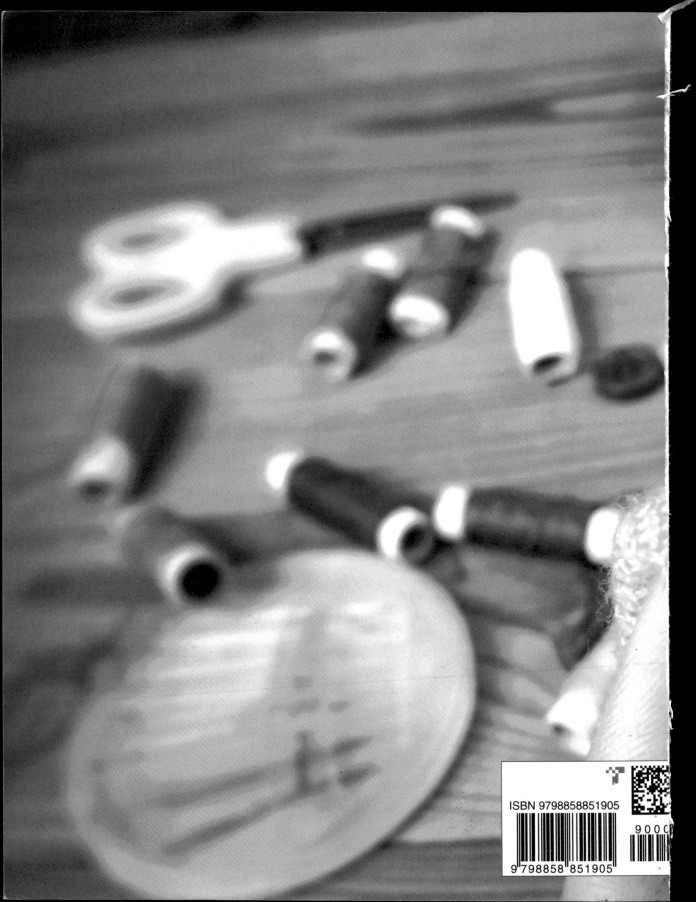

ISBN 9798858851905